★CRIME FILES★
Roy Apps

WORLD CUP HEIST

illustrated by Kevin Hopgood

W
FRANKLIN WATTS
LONDON•SYDNEY

First published in 2007 by
Franklin Watts
338 Euston Road
London NW1 3BH

Franklin Watts Australia
Level 17/207 Kent Street
Sydney NSW 2000

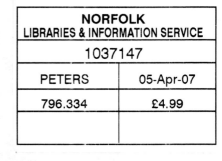
Text © Roy Apps 2007
Illustrations © Franklin Watts 2007

A CIP catalogue record for this book
is available from the British Library.

ISBN: 978 0 7496 7057 3

Dewey Classification: 823.914

Illustrator: Kevin Hopgood
Series editor: Adrian Cole
Reading consultant: Prue Goodwin, Lecturer at the
National Centre for Language and Literacy, Reading
Art director and cover designer: Jonathan Hair

Cover photo © UPP/Topfoto

Printed in Great Britain by Bookmarque Ltd, Croydon

Franklin Watts is a division of
Hachette Children's Books.

A note from the author:
Crime Files are true
stories, but some
of the events on
which they are based
have been dramatised
and edited.

Contents

1: World Cup fever

In March 1966, England buzzed with World Cup fever. The tournament was being held in England. For two weeks before the football matches started, the Jules Rimet Trophy – the original World Cup – was being shown at an exhibition in London.

On the first Sunday of the exhibition,
two men walked down a road in
Westminster. It was a bright morning
and they were going to the pub for a
lunchtime pint – and to collect some
forged World Cup tickets.

As they passed a church hall, a poster caught their attention.

'They've never put the World Cup on display in a stamp exhibition?' said the scruffy-looking man.

'There's only one way to find out,' replied his friend.

They opened the door to the church hall
and went in. All around the walls stood
glass cases full of stamps. And right
in the middle of the room was a table.
On the table was the Jules Rimet Trophy.
There wasn't a guard
in sight.

'That's criminal, leaving the World Cup unguarded like that. Why, it's just asking to be nicked,' said the scruffy man.

'You're right,' said his friend as he lifted the trophy, rolled it up in his Sunday paper and stuffed it inside his jacket. It was as easy as that. There wasn't an alarm ringing anywhere!

The two men walked out of the church hall as casually as they had walked in. Then, instead of going to the pub, they headed straight home.

'What have we done?'

'Nicked the World Cup,' said the man with the bulging jacket.

'And what are we going to do now?'

'I don't know,' he said, shaking his head. 'I really don't know.'

2: Plan of action

The crooks who had stolen the World Cup may not have known what to do, but the police were clear about their plan of action.

'We've got to keep this quiet for as long as possible. When the public hear that the World Cup is missing, we'll be a laughing stock,' said the superintendent.

The boss of the security firm in charge of guarding the World Cup was in deep trouble. His men, who should have been guarding the trophy, were off having a tea break when it was stolen.

The board of the Football Association were embarrassed, but they were also very worried. The World Cup tournament was due to start in a couple of weeks. Without the Jules Rimet Trophy to present to the winning team, how could there be a World Cup?

Denis Follows was the secretary of the Football Association. As he drove home from a meeting with the police, he thought long and hard. The Jules Rimet Trophy was £30,000 worth of solid gold. He believed that a criminal gang would melt it down and sell the gold through underworld contacts.

Instead of driving straight home, Denis Follows went to a shop in East London called 'George Bird. Silversmith'. He checked to make sure that he hadn't been tailed. Then he got out of his car and knocked on the front door of the shop.

A small, elderly man opened the door and beckoned Follows into the shop.

'I want you to make a replica of the Jules Rimet Trophy,' Follows told George Bird.

'Why?' asked the puzzled silversmith.

'Never mind why,' replied Follows.

'It's going to cost you,' said Bird.

'Money is not a problem,' said Follows. 'You've got just 12 weeks to do the job. And remember, not a word to anyone.'

By the next day, when George Bird had started making his replica World Cup, news of the theft of the original trophy was already in the newspapers.

READ ALL ABOUT IT!

The story made headlines all over the world. The superintendent was right. The police, the Football Association and the security firm were a complete laughing stock. Leaving the World Cup unguarded in a church hall? It was incredible!

3: Mystery caller

Soon the police were swamped with letters and telephone calls from people who said they knew the location of the World Cup. Detective Inspector Len Buggy from the Flying Squad was sent in to sort out the mess. He and two detectives began to follow up the hundreds of letters and calls.

But there was no sign of the World Cup.

Then, two days after the theft, a man called Joe Mears received a telephone call he hadn't been expecting. Mears was the Chairman of the Football Association and of Chelsea Football Club.

'Mr Mears?' said a voice on the other end of the line. The voice was muffled, but it was definitely a man with a London accent. 'Now, listen carefully...'

'I'm listening,' said Mears.

'Good. There will be a parcel at
Chelsea Football Club tomorrow.
Follow the instructions inside.'
Then the man hung up.

The next day, a parcel marked 'Urgent.
Private and Confidential' arrived for
Joe Mears. He took it into his office
and locked the door.

Inside the parcel was the lid of the solid gold Jules Rimet Trophy. There was also a note.

Dear Joe

No doubt you view with very much concern the loss of the World Cup. To me, it is only so much scrap gold. If I don't hear from you by Thursday or Friday at the latest, I assume it is one for the POT.

Joe Mears had hardly finished reading the note when his phone rang.

'Mr Mears? I hope the parcel arrived safely. Now, all you have to do to get the rest of it is meet me in Battersea Park on Friday with £15,000. The cup will arrive by cab on Saturday. Put a note in the *London Evening News* to confirm. And on no account contact the police. Got it?'

'Who are you?' asked Joe Mears.

But the phone line was already dead.

A small advert appeared in the Thursday edition of the *London Evening News*:

> ```
> Willing to do business.
> Joe.
> ```

The same day, the telephone rang in Inspector Len Buggy's office.

'Inspector? It's Joe Mears here. We need to talk. Urgently.'

Joe Mears had ignored the warning from the mysterious caller and had contacted the police.

4: The meeting

The next day, the Friday after the theft,
Joe Mears's car could be seen driving
through Battersea Park. On the back
seat was a suitcase. It contained £500
in used notes. The rest of the ransom,
£14,500, was made up from cut-out bits
of old newspaper.

The driver of the car got out,
but it was Detective Inspector
Buggy, not Joe Mears!

A tall man wearing a large overcoat approached him.

'Joe Mears?' asked the man.

Inspector Buggy shook his head. 'No, I'm his assistant, Mr McPhee,' he lied.

'Get in the car, McPhee,' ordered the man, 'and start driving.' The man sat in the front passenger seat. Inspector Buggy got back in the car and pulled away slowly.

'Where are we going?' Buggy asked.

'Never you mind,' replied the man.
'Just keep driving.'

'The money's all there,' lied Buggy,
nodding towards the back seat.

The man didn't seem to hear. While Buggy drove on, the man was busy looking out of the window and checking the mirrors. Then he swore under his breath. 'You double-crossing little toerag! I told Joe Mears, no police!'

'Police? I can't see any police,' said Inspector Buggy.

'That blue van behind us,' said the man. 'It's been there since we left Battersea Park. I know a police van when I see one! Pull over now!'

Buggy screeched over to the kerb. The man leapt out of the passenger door before the car came to a standstill. Behind him, the doors of the blue van flew open and six police officers jumped out and charged down the pavement. The man was on the ground and in handcuffs before you could say *Match of the Day*.

'Gotcha!' yelled Inspector Buggy, triumphantly.

'Yeah, but you haven't got the World Cup, have you?' the man in handcuffs snarled.

At Rochester Row police station, the police discovered that the man's name was Edward Betchley. He was a small-time crook with a previous conviction for receiving stolen tins of corned beef.

'Look, I didn't nick the World Cup.
I'm just the middleman. But I'll do
a deal with you,' he told Buggy.

'You let my girlfriend visit me in
Brixton Prison – without the warders
being there – and I promise you'll get
the World Cup back.'

Inspector Buggy wanted to tell Betchley to forget it. But it was now almost a week since the World Cup had been stolen. The police and the Football Association were desperate. As each day passed, the date of the World Cup tournament got closer and closer.

'Okay, Betchley,' sighed Inspector Buggy. 'You've got a deal.'

The following afternoon, Betchley's girlfriend visited him in prison.
No warders were present.

At the end of visiting time, Inspector Buggy watched the woman go. He shook his head, impatiently. Could Betchley be trusted? Would the World Cup be found? There was no way to know. All the police could do now was wait.

5: A lucky find

Two days later, a man named David Corbett left his South London flat to go to the phone box. With him was his dog, Pickles. Originally, the dog had belonged to his brother. But Pickles loved to chew furniture, and just about everything else, so David's brother had thrown him out. Now Pickles belonged to David.

David lived with his wife and young daughter. David's wife didn't really like Pickles. He was a scruffy mongrel and was always causing trouble – and he kept chewing things!

As David opened the front gate, Pickles pulled excitedly on his lead.

'Stop that, Pickles!' said David, firmly.

But Pickles didn't stop pulling. He pulled David towards the front wheel of next door's car and started pawing at something.

'What have you got there then, boy?'

Whatever it was, it had been tightly wrapped in newspaper. David picked it up and ripped off some of the paper. Inside there was a statue of a woman holding a dish over her head. The statue was inscribed with the words 'Germany, Uruguay, Brazil'.

'No, it can't be!' David exclaimed in disbelief. He held on to the statue tightly and rushed indoors to his wife, with Pickles at his heels.

'Look what Pickles has found!'
he shouted.

David's wife wasn't a football fan and didn't know the difference between the World Cup and a teacup. 'Where on earth did he dig that thing up?' she asked.

'It was under next door's car,' said David, excitedly. 'It's the Jules Rimet Trophy!'

'The what?'

'The World Cup!' exclaimed David.

'Don't talk daft,' said David's wife. 'What would a World Cup be doing under next door's car?'

'The thieves must have put it there,' replied David.

'But why?' asked his wife. 'A bit of a silly place to hide a World Cup, isn't it?'

David shrugged. 'The important thing is, Pickles has found it! Our dog is a superstar!'

6: Star performance

Next day, photographs of Pickles
appeared in all the newspapers. He was
on television and he even appeared on
Blue Peter.

Pickles and David watched the World Cup
final on television. They saw England
beat Germany 4–2. David cheered and
Pickles barked loudly as the Queen
presented England's captain, Bobby
Moore, with the Jules Rimet Trophy.

After the match, Bobby Moore and the
team began their lap of honour around
Wembley Stadium. Running with them
was a man in a grey suit. He was Bob
Geggie, and he was a plain-clothes police
officer. The Football Association weren't
taking any more chances. They were
making sure that the World Cup was
not stolen again.

The team left the pitch and jogged back through the tunnel towards the dressing room. Just then, another police officer approached the England defender, Nobby Stiles, who was holding the Cup.

'I'll take that,' he said. 'You can have this one.'

The police officer took the World Cup from Nobby Stiles and gave him a replica in its place. It was the one made by silversmith George Bird for the Football Association secretary, Denis Follows. The officer handed the real Jules Rimet Trophy to officials from the Football Association, who put it under lock and key until the next World Cup in 1970.

The 1970 World Cup was won by Brazil, who were given the Jules Rimet Trophy permanently because they had won the tournament three times.

In 1983 the Jules Rimet Trophy was stolen again, this time in Brazil, and has never been seen since.

i: Crime Files appendix

* Who stole the World Cup?

To this day, no one has ever discovered who actually stole the Jules Rimet Trophy from the stamp exhibition. The only description the police had was of a man in his early 30s, of average height, with greased black hair, and possibly a scar on his face.

* Pickles

Pickles became 'Dog of the Year' and won a year's supply of dog food. Sadly, he died in 1967 after an accident.

* David Corbett, the owner of Pickles

David was questioned by police, before he received the cash reward of £3,000 for finding the missing trophy.

* Edward Betchley, the middleman

Edward was convicted of demanding money with menaces and sentenced to two years in prison. He died shortly after his release.

* Joe Mears, Chairman of the FA

Joe died in 1966 before any of the World Cup matches were played.

* The Jules Rimet Trophy

Jules Rimet was President of the World Football Federation from 1921–54.
The Cup was originally called 'Victory', but was renamed after Jules Rimet suggested holding an international football competition. It stood 35cm high and weighed 3.8 kilograms.

* The replica

George Bird's replica of the Jules Rimet Trophy was sold at auction in 1997 for £254,000. It is now at the National Football Museum in Preston, Lancashire.

ii: Word file

Crook – a word sometimes used to describe a thief or dishonest person.

Detective – a police officer who works in a team to solve crimes.

Flying Squad – a small team of police officers that responds quickly to serious crimes.

Middleman – someone who receives stolen goods, but doesn't steal them.

Mongrel – a mixed-breed dog.

Ransom – an amount of money that must be paid for the return of something.

Replica – an exact copy.

Tailed – when someone is followed.

Under lock and key – when something is kept in a secure place.

Underworld – the world of thieves and crooks.

Used notes – bank notes that are harder for police to trace because they do not run in serial number order.

iii: Crime Files weblinks

http://news.bbc.co.uk/onthisday/hi/dates/stories/march/20/newsid_2861000/2861545.stm

This is a page of the BBC news archive where you can find a copy of the news article and a video clip about the 1966 World Cup heist.

http://www.nationalfootballmuseum.com/

Find out what's happening at the National Football Museum – and see photographs of the Jules Rimet Trophy.

http://observer.guardian.co.uk/sport/story/0,,1759464,00.html

A report on the theft of the Jules Rimet Trophy from the *Observer*.

http://www.fifa.com/en/history/history/0,1283,1,00.html

The history of football and the World Cup on the official FIFA website.

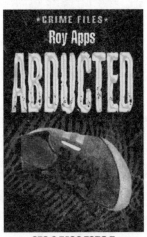